Date: 11/20/20

J 595.789 YOR
York, M. J.,
Butterflies and moths /

BUTTERFLIES AND MOTHS

BY M. J. YORK

Published by The Child's World®
1980 Lookout Drive • Mankato, MN 56003-1705
800-599-READ • www.childsworld.com

Photographs ©: S. W. Olson/iStockphoto, cover
(butterfly), 2, 8, 20, 24 (butterfly); iStockphoto,
cover (moth), 3, 16, 21, 24 (moth); Leena Robinson/
Shutterstock Images, 4; Shaun Wilkinson/Shutterstock
Images, 6; Pieter Bruin/Shutterstock Images, 9; Andy
Murrr/Shutterstock Images, 10; Henrik Larsson/
Shutterstock Images, 13; Shutterstock Images, 14, 17;
Steven R. Smith/Shutterstock Images, 19

ISBN 9781503835870
LCCN 2019942999

Printed in the United States of America

ABOUT THE AUTHOR

M. J. York is a children's author
and editor living in Minnesota.
She loves learning about
different animals.

TABLE OF CONTENTS

Fluttery Bug

An **insect** flutters past. It lands on a flower. It has four wings. It has six legs. **Antennae** sprout from its head. Is it a butterfly or a moth? How are they different?

Both moths and butterflies get food from flowers.

Each kind of butterfly has a different wing pattern.

Butterflies

Butterflies have four wings. The wings have tiny **scales**. Most butterflies have scales of different, bright colors. This can form patterns. The colors warn **predators** to stay away. The colors help other butterflies find them.

Butterflies close their wings when they rest. They can move each wing separately.

Most butterflies come out during the day. Butterflies use their antennae to smell. The antennae also help them balance. Butterfly antennae have a small round tip called a club.

Butterflies have many uses for their antennae.

Caterpillars change into butterflies while inside their chrysalises.

Butterflies go through a change called **metamorphosis**. A caterpillar hatches from an egg. It eats and grows. Then it attaches to a plant or a wall. Its skin splits open. Underneath the skin is a **chrysalis**. It is a hard, smooth shell. Inside the insect is changing. When it comes out, it is a butterfly.

Moths

Moths have four wings. Many have dull or plain colors. Moths fold their wings down on their bodies. Or they keep their wings open when resting. Their front wings are attached to their back wings.

Moths are not usually as brightly colored as butterflies.

Some moth antennae
look like combs.

14

Most moths come out at night.
They have big antennae. Usually the
antennae look feathery or furry. Moths
need a good sense of smell in the dark.
They find each other by scent.

Moths also go through
metamorphosis. But their process is
a bit different from butterflies. They
hatch from eggs as caterpillars. The
caterpillar grows, then it hangs upside
down. It wraps itself in silk. This is its
cocoon. Inside, it turns into a moth.

Moths make the silk they use for their cocoons.

17

What's the Difference?

Butterflies fly during the day. Moths fly at night. Butterflies are colorful. Moths are usually plain. Butterflies have thin antennae with a club. Moths have feathery antennae. Butterflies rest with their wings together. Moths often keep their wings open or folded down.

Some moths have bright colors, such as the Luna moth.

Their metamorphosis is different, too. Butterflies change in a chrysalis. Moths change in a cocoon.

Butterflies and moths have a lot in common. They are closely related. And they are all amazing!

BUTTERFLIES

Club on antennae

Can move wings separately

- Build a chrysalis
- Come out during the day
- Rest with wings together

Bright colors

MOTHS

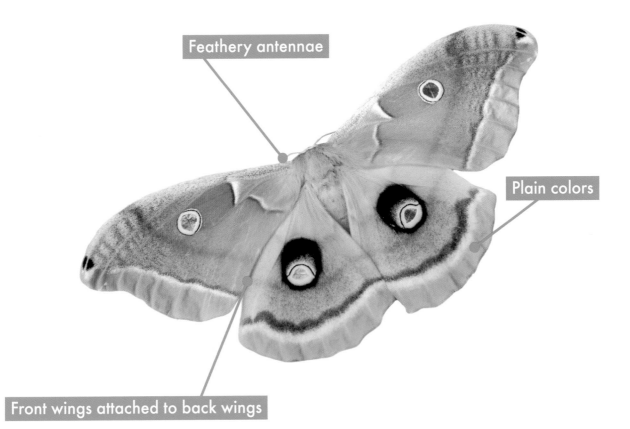

Feathery antennae

Plain colors

Front wings attached to back wings

- Build a cocoon
- Come out at night
- Rest with wings open and down

GLOSSARY

antennae (an-TEN-ee) Antennae are feelers on insects' heads. Butterflies and moths use antennae to sense around them.

chrysalis (KRIS-uh-lis) A chrysalis is a hard shell that protects a caterpillar as it turns into a butterfly. The chrysalis was attached to a tree.

cocoon (kuh-KOON) A cocoon is the silk wrapping that protects a caterpillar as it turns into a moth. The cocoon hung from a branch.

insect (IN-sekt) An insect is a bug that has six legs and often has wings. A butterfly is an insect.

metamorphosis (met-uh-MOR-fuh-sis) Metamorphosis is the set of changes an insect goes through in its life cycle from egg to butterfly or moth. The caterpillar prepared to go through metamorphosis.

predators (PRED-uh-turs) Predators are animals that hunt and eat other animals. Birds are predators of butterflies and moths.

scales (SKAYLZ) Scales on butterflies and moths are tiny overlapping pieces that form the surface of their wings. Scales make the butterflies' beautiful patterns.

TO LEARN MORE

IN THE LIBRARY
Herrington, Lisa M. *Butterflies and Moths*. New York, NY: Children's Press, 2016.

Mattern, Joanne. *Butterflies and Moths*. Egremont, MA: Red Chair Press, 2017.

Reinke, Beth Bence. *Where Did the Caterpillar Go?* Mankato, MN:
The Child's World, 2017.

ON THE WEB
Visit our website for links about butterflies and moths:
childsworld.com/links

*Note to Parents, Teachers, and Librarians: We routinely verify our Web links to make sure
they are safe and active sites. So encourage your readers to check them out!*

Draw a picture of a butterfly and a moth. Your picture should clearly show the differences between the butterfly and the moth. Look at pages 20 and 21 for help.

INDEX